Did You

LANCA...

A MISCELLANY

Compiled by Julia Skinner

With particular reference to the work of Clive Hardy, Cliff Hayes,
Dennis & Jan Kelsall and Robert Swain

THE FRANCIS FRITH COLLECTION

www.francisfrith.com

First published in the United Kingdom in 2012 by The Francis Frith Collection®

This edition published exclusively for Bradwell Books in 2012
For trade enquiries see: www.bradwellbooks.com or tel: 0800 834 920
ISBN 978-1-84589-686-7

British Library Cataloguing in Publication Data

Did You Know? Lancashire - A Miscellany
Compiled by Julia Skinner
With particular reference to the work of Clive Hardy, Cliff Hayes, Dennis & Jan Kelsall
and Robert Swain

The Francis Frith Collection
Oakley Business Park,
Wylye Road, Dinton,
Wiltshire SP3 5EU
Tel: +44 (0) 1722 716 376
Email: info@francisfrith.co.uk
www.francisfrith.com

Printed and bound in Malaysia
Contains material sourced from responsibly managed forests

Front Cover: **BLACKBURN, CORPORATION PARK, THE ENTRANCE 1895** 35729p
Frontispiece: **NEWTON, THE VILLAGE 1921** 71218
Contents: **EARBY, WATER STREET c1900** E160301

The colour-tinting is for illustrative purposes only, and is not intended to be historically accurate

CONTENTS

INTRODUCTION

Described in a 1930s guidebook to England as one of the richest counties in the land, Lancashire was then, and still is, rightly deserving of such praise. The region's richness extends far beyond the industrial and commercial wealth that the author of the time had in mind, for Lancashire's borders encompass a surprising diversity and interest in its cities, towns, villages and countryside that few other regions equal. True, the south and east can hardly be described as 'pretty', but the towns, which were the birthplace of the Industrial Revolution, have other qualities which make them worthy of investigation. The profits generated by their factories and mills were vast, and the investments in civic and commercial building that followed produced some of the 18th and 19th centuries' most eloquent architectural statements. Those towns were also cradles of cultural development, for in them were established many fine museums and art galleries. In dramatic contrast, Lancashire's wild countryside can sometimes seem as remote as anywhere – a person can roam all day across the moors, hardly meeting another along the way.

The industries which brought wealth to Lancashire's industrial towns also triggered the development of the county's coastal holiday resorts. The 18th century had seen the popularisation of sea-cures and therapies amongst the middle and upper classes but, until the railway age, ordinary working people had neither the time nor money to visit the seaside. However, with the advent of relatively cheap rail travel, people flocked there in their thousands from the industrial towns, and so began the tradition of an annual break from the toil and drudgery of the mills and factories. Resorts competed to attract customers, building ever more impressive promenades, piers, pavilions, theatres and other places of entertainment, a race that culminated in the construction of one of the iconic buildings of Lancashire – the famous Blackpool Tower.

The border separating Lancashire from its neighbours traces a meandering line across windswept, lonely hills and vast, open moors. Before the local government reorganisation of 1974, the county stretched from the Three Counties Stone at the top of the Wrynose Path, now in Cumbria, to the River Mersey, south of Manchester. That Westmorland apparently isolated Furness from the rest of Lancashire was not an anomaly, since the two had been linked since antiquity by the vast expanse of sand revealed each time the tide retreated from Morecambe Bay. Today, the county is much reduced. 'Lancashire across the sands' and much of the large conurbations of Merseyside and Manchester (including Manchester, Liverpool, Wigan, Eccles, Rochdale, Bolton, and Bury) have been lost to the new metropolitan counties of Greater Manchester and Merseyside, and the border with Lancashire's long-standing rival, Yorkshire, has been redrawn.

DUNSOP BRIDGE, HODDER BRIDGE 1921 71220

LANCASHIRE DIALECT WORDS AND PHRASES

'Appen' - maybe, perhaps.

'Ar Peg' - my wife.

'Attercop' - a spider.

'Barmpot' - a simpleton.

'Bicker' - to argue.

'Blobbers' - bubbles.

'Brast' - burst.

'Champion' - good, well.

'Chunner' - grumble.

'Claggy' - sticky, as in mud.

'Corporation pop' - water.

'Dule' - the Devil (from **'th' owd lad'**).

'Flummoxed' - confused, puzzled.

'Gawmless' - daft, silly.

'Ginnel' - a narrow passageway between houses.

'Jannock' - straightforward, genuine.

'Jiggered' - exhausted, or broken, not working.

'Lugs' - ears.

'Mawkin' - dirty.

'Moither' - annoy, as in **'stop moitherin' me'** - stop annoying me.

'Motty' - a small sum of money.

'Parky' - cold.

'Yutick' or **'Utick'** - a Lancashire dialect word for the stonechat, a small bird.

Preston is famous for its Guilds. Since the early 16th century Guild celebrations (the 'Preston Guild') have been held every 20 years, hence the Lancashire saying **'Every Preston Guild'**, which means 'not very often'. The celebrations take place over a full year, with one week being the main Guild Week when colourful processions are held, along with spectacular indoor and outdoor events, street parties, concerts and exhibitions.

HAUNTED LANCASHIRE

The Sun Inn at Chipping in the Ribble Valley is reputed to be haunted by the ghost of Lizzie Dean, who worked there in the 1830s. She was seduced by a local man who promised to marry her, but he jilted her and married her best friend. On the day of their wedding Lizzie hanged herself in the attic of the inn.

It is said that 16th-century Borwick Hall near Carnforth is haunted by a ghostly White Lady, and that anyone sleeping lengthways in the Coffin Room never wakes up…

Blackpool Tower is said to be haunted by the ghosts of two clowns from the Tower Circus, Doodles and Charlie Cairoli, whose distinctive laugh has been heard there; the Ghost Train at the Pleasure Beach at Blackpool may be haunted by a real ghost – the sound of unexplained heavy footsteps has been heard there, believed to be caused by the ghost of a former ride operator called Cloggy, who always wore clogs; and a phantom tram is said to glide along the rails on Blackpool's seafront at night.

Samlesbury Old Hall near Preston was the home of the Roman Catholic de Southworth family, and is said to be haunted by the weeping ghost of Dorothy Southworth. She fell in love with a Protestant neighbour, but the pair were forbidden to marry by their families because of religious differences. Dorothy's brothers killed her lover before her eyes, and her heartbroken spirit haunts the hall and its grounds.

The spirit of the executed Roman Catholic priest St John Wall may haunt Chingle Hall at Goosnarth, responsible for doors mysteriously opening, tapping noises on walls, and the sound of footsteps tramping through 'The Haunted Room', where sightings of a ghostly monk have been reported. Dogs frequently stand up to watch something passing through the downstairs rooms which is invisible to humans around them. Visitors have also reported feeling someone tugging at their clothes or holding their hand in 'Eleanor's Room', where a young girl was held captive for twelve years before she died.

LANCASHIRE MISCELLANY

In the first century AD the Romans built a fort at what is now Lancaster, above a crossing point of the River Lon, or Lune. The name of the fort is not known, but the Roman word for fort, 'castra', became 'ceaster' in Anglo-Saxon, so the fort on the Lon became 'Lonceaster', and then over time 'Lancaster'.

In 1199 Lancaster received its first royal charter from King John. This gave Lancaster's burgesses some special privileges, including permission to take wood from the forest of Quernmore for building, and the right to graze their animals in the forest as far from the town as they could return home within the day.

De Vitre Street in Lancaster is named after Dr Edward De Vitre, who did much work to help the mentally impaired in Lancashire. He was instrumental in setting up the Royal Albert Hospital in Ashton Road in Lancaster. When it opened in 1870 it was one of only 4 regional institutions in England set up specifically for the care and education of children with learning disabilities. The Grade II listed hospital building still stands, but is now used for other educational purposes.

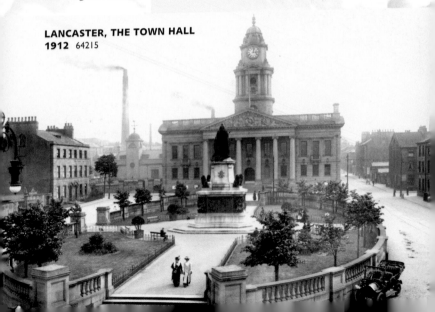

LANCASTER, THE TOWN HALL
1912 64215

LANCASTER, THE CASTLE FROM ST MARY'S CHURCH 1886 18084

The Norman knight Roger of Poitou began to build a stone castle in Lancaster in the late 11th century, and a stone keep was added in the late 12th century. Only parts of the old building remain, mainly the Norman keep and Adrian's Tower (or Hadrian's Tower). The gatehouse entrance was added c1400. After the Civil War much of the castle was demolished, but the parts used for the courts and the prison were retained, leaving the gatehouse and the buildings on the south and west sides. Visitors can tour the castle today and see the condemned cell, an early gallows and (in the Crown Court) the branding iron used in past times when a prisoner was found guilty of a crime. The red-hot iron applied the letter 'M' to the prisoner's hand, for 'malefactor', or evil-doer. The mark was permanent, and showed that the person had been before the courts.

Several ghosts are reputed to roam Lancaster Castle – a child, an old hag, a not-so-old woman, and a spectral monk – and visitors on guided tours around the building sometimes report a feeling of being pushed by an invisible hand.

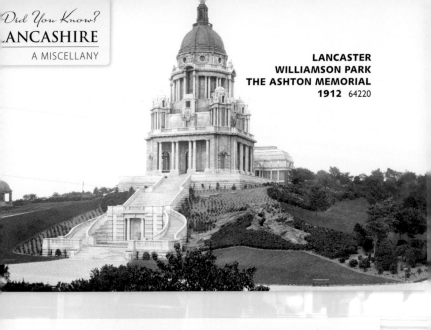

LANCASTER
WILLIAMSON PARK
THE ASHTON MEMORIAL
1912 64220

Lancaster became wealthy in Georgian times, resulting in the erection of fine buildings, many of which still stand today. Stone from local quarries was readily available, in particular where polished freestone was needed (sandstone rubbed to a flat finish). This stone appears 'veined', caused by iron impurities in the stone causing brownish streaks.

Williamson Park in Lancaster was begun in the 1860s as a work scheme for the unemployed; they were to turn the bleak moorland and the quarries that had once provided so much stone for the building of Lancaster into a charming and interesting park. James Williamson paid for the park, and his son (also James), later Lord Ashton and known as 'the linoleum king', carried on the support and built the Ashton Memorial there to commemorate his second wife, Jessie, who died in 1904 (photograph 64220, above). The Taj Mahal of Lancaster, its green copper-domed roof dominates the highest spot over the city.

Lancaster's impressive Queen Victoria Monument in Dalton Square (photograph 64217x, below) represents the queen guarded by four bronze lions. Commemorated in the panels below are worthies from her reign, including Lord Derby, Robert Peel, Richard Cobden, John Bright, William Makepeace Thackeray, Alfred, Lord Tennyson, and Lancaster-born Richard Owen, the biologist who coined the word 'dinosauria' ('terrible reptile'); there are forty people in all, but only two women, Florence Nightingale and Mary Ann Evans, who wrote novels under the name George Eliot. The four corner pieces represent Truth, Wisdom, Justice and Freedom.

By the 1750s, Lancaster was the fourth busiest port in the country, but the River Lune was silting up, causing problems in getting goods into and out of Lancaster. The solution was to build a three-acre dock near the village of Glasson. By 1791 it was a fully operational port, and warehouse offices and a custom house sprang up around the quayside, with cottages nearby for the stevedores who handled the cargoes.

**LANCASTER
THE QUEEN VICTORIA
MONUMENT 1912**
64217x

The Lancaster Canal followed a route surveyed by John Rennie from West Houghton in south Lancashire to Kendal. Construction began in 1793, and in 1794 work started on the 600ft-long Lune aqueduct. Rennie wanted this built in brick but the Canal Committee preferred stone, which so increased that too little money was left to cross the River Ribble – there was no link by water between the Ribble and the main canal system until the opening of the Millennium Ribble Link in 2002. The Lancaster Canal was formally opened between Preston and Tewitfield in 1797, and in 1819 was opened right through to Kendal, but it was not until 1826 that the Glasson Arm was completed, linking the canal with the sea via Glasson Dock, where a huge basin was built to accommodate the barges that transported the cargoes inland. In photograph 68306x (below) we see typical barge propulsion on the canal at Carnforth, towards the northern end of the canal; the top section was abandoned after the M6 motorway was built.

CARNFORTH
A BARGE ON THE CANAL
1918 68306x

CARNFORTH MARKET STREET 1898 41032

Carnforth's industries of sand and gravel extraction and iron smelting depended upon the Lancaster Canal and later the railway. The Furness & Midland Railway and the London & North Western Railway opened Carnforth Station between them in 1880, and it became an important junction. The station was used as a set in the film 'Brief Encounter'.

Just north of Carnforth is Warton, which is famous for its American connections. Ancestors of George Washington (the first President of the USA) came to live in Warton in the 13th century, and at a later time in the Middle Ages one of them helped financially towards the building of the tower of St Oswald's Church in the village. A stone carving of the Washington family crest used to be displayed on the tower, but it is now kept inside the church; it features stars and stripes (three 'mullets' and two 'bars'), and is believed to have been the inspiration for the American flag, the Stars and Stripes, which is now flown from the church tower on every 4th of July, Independence Day in the States.

COWAN BRIDGE, WHERE CHARLOTTE BRONTE WENT TO SCHOOL 1926 79108

Cowan Bridge near the Cumbrian border is where the author Charlotte Bronte and her sisters Maria, Elizabeth and Emily attended the former Clergy Daughters' School in 1824-25 (photograph 79108, above). They experienced such spartan conditions there that Maria and Elizabeth died as a result. Charlotte Bronte recalled the sisters' unhappy experiences at Cowan Bridge when she used the school as the basis for Lowood School in her novel 'Jane Eyre'.

Lancashire was shaken by several earthquakes in the 19th century. The 'Lancaster earthquake' occurred in August 1835; the 'Irish Sea earthquake' occurred in April 1843, when tremors were felt over a wide area, including Northern Ireland, the Isle of Man and north-west England, and further tremors were recorded in March 1869 and March 1871.

The rivers Leven, Kent, Keer, Lune and Wyre drain into Morecambe Bay, which is the largest expanse of intertidal mudflats and sand in Britain. It is one of Europe's best habitats for migrating birds, but its quicksand and fast-moving tides can make it a dangerous place for humans. The seaside town of Morecambe is situated on the southern end of Morecambe Bay. Morecambe was originally called Poulton, but to avoid confusion with another Poulton near Blackpool (Poulton-le-Fylde), it became Poulton-le-Sands. Poulton-le-Sands and the nearby villages of Bare and Torrisholme came together to form Morecambe around 1860. There were two piers at Morecambe in the past. Central Pier opened in 1869, but without kiosks or pavilions at the end – its attraction was that holidaymakers could walk over the water and look down on the sea. In 1896 Morecambe opened a second pier, West End Pier (see photograph 37387, below). The building of a lavish pavilion at the end of West End Pier motivated the building of an Indian-style pavilion and theatre at the end of Central Pier, nicknamed 'the Taj Mahal of Morecambe'. The West End Pier was mainly destroyed in a storm in November 1977, and was demolished soon after.

MORECAMBE, THE WEST END PIER 1896 37387

LANCASHIRE
A MISCELLANY

St Patrick himself is said to have been shipwrecked on Heysham Head, south of Morecambe, at the beginning of the fifth century, whilst attempting to reach Scotland from Ireland. In later years monks from Ireland built a chapel there in his memory; the now-ruined chapel dates from the eighth century, and is the only example left in England of a single-cell Saxon chapel.

Also of historic interest at Heysham Head is the 10th-century Hogback Stone, shown in photograph 64232 (below) in 1912 when it was sited in St Peter's churchyard. The stone marked the grave of a Viking warrior who had converted to Christianity, but although one side of the stone is carved with Christian symbols, the other side represents the pagan heaven, Valhalla. The Hogback Stone is now kept inside the church to preserve it. There are other hogback stones in Britain, but this is the finest.

HEYSHAM, ST PETER'S CHURCHYARD, THE HOGBACK STONE 1912
64232

FLEETWOOD, THE BEACH AND LOWER LIGHTHOUSE 1892 30421

Fleetwood was once an important deep-sea fishing centre, a tourist resort and a busy port that handled passengers and cargo bound for Ireland, the Isle of Man and Glasgow. Fleetwood was a 'new town' developed from 1836 on the estate owned by Peter Fleetwood-Hesketh. The oldest surviving building in the town now houses Fleetwood Museum on Queen's Terrace, which tells the story of Fleetwood's fishing heritage. Fleetwood's deep-sea fishing industry once employed over 4,000 local men and boys, but it declined in the 1970s when local trawlers lost their fishing grounds in the North Atlantic. Fleetwood commemorates its fishing heritage with a pair of bronze figures on the promenade, representing a woman and child looking out to sea and welcoming the fishermen home. The figures were donated by a local company that developed from the fishing industry – Fisherman's Friend, which makes its famous menthol lozenges in the town. The lozenges originated in Fleetwood in the 1860s when local pharmacist James Lofthouse made them as an aid to deep-sea fishermen who suffered various respiratory problems whilst working in the extreme conditions of the icy fishing grounds.

POULTON-LE-FYLDE, THE MARKET PLACE, THE STOCKS 1895 35617

Fleetwood is famous for its two prominent lighthouses designed by the great architect Decimus Burton, the Lower (or Beach) Lighthouse (the neo-classical building seen in the centre of photograph 30421 (on page 15) and the Upper Lighthouse, both of which became operational in 1840 to mark a safe passage into Fleetwood's harbour, and which are both still functioning lighthouses. The Lower Lighthouse on the seafront is 13 metres (44 feet) high, and approaching ships set a course lining it with the second light, which lies just inland. The Upper Lighthouse, which stands 29 metres (93 feet) tall, is popularly known as the Pharos because it was modelled on the famous Pharos lighthouse in Alexandria in Egypt. The Pharos is unusual because it is it the only still-functioning lighthouse in Britain that stands in the middle of a residential street – Pharos Street – where it now forms a traffic roundabout.

The coastal plain region of western Lancashire known as 'The Fylde' gets its name from a Scandinavian word meaning 'field'. The productive agricultural land of this area also gave it the name of 'the breadbasket of Lancashire' in the past. As time went on, statuesque tower mills to grind corn replaced the old wooden peg mills of the region, and 'Windmill Land' became another apt description for the Fylde. However, the only working windmill left in the Fylde is Marsh Mill at Thornton Cleveleys (see photograph T307001, below). Marsh Mill is a large Fylde-type brick tower mill with four patent shuttered sails and a fantail. Dated 1794, it worked commercially until 1922. This photograph shows the mill in a disused condition before restoration work began. It is now conserved in complete working order, and is open to visitors.

Photograph 35617 (opposite) shows examples of both punishment and commerce 'local style' in the past – the stocks, whipping post, fish stones and market cross in the market place at Poulton-le-Fylde were described in the 18th century as 'the most complete example of their kind in England'.

**THORNTON
CLEVELEYS
MARSH MILL
c1955** T307001

BLACKPOOL, THE WINTER GARDENS 1890 22892

The coming of the railway in 1846 sparked Blackpool's growth into a major holiday resort, and thousands of factory and mill workers flocked there each summer from northern industrial towns. The resort was developed along mainly down-to-earth lines, and when it opened in 1878 the Winter Gardens was probably Blackpool's last throw at catering for a sophisticated audience. It housed a library, reading room, art gallery and concert hall. The Floral Hall, a pavilion seating 3,000 people, and the Empress Ballroom were added soon after, and it became a major attraction. However, the acoustics were very poor. When the great actress Sarah Bernhardt was engaged to play in 'The Lady of the Camellias' there in 1882, she had so much difficulty making herself heard that she walked out at the end of the first act and never went back, offended by the cries of 'Speak up, lass!' from the audience, who had paid good money to see her and wanted their money's worth. The writing was on the wall for cultural pursuits as early as Whit weekend 1879, when the principal attraction at the Winter Gardens was a young woman being fired from a cannon.

In the 1890s, in an unusual publicity stunt, 100 parrots were trained to screech about the delights of Blackpool's Winter Gardens and left in hotels and restaurants around Lancashire.

There was much investment in the resort's attractions as Blackpool grew in popularity, with the establishment of no less than three piers. Doubling as a landing stage for steamers, North Pier was the first of Blackpool's three piers to be built, and opened in 1863. Work began on Blackpool's second pier, then called the South Jetty, in 1867 (photograph 53855, below); it was renamed Central Pier when the resort's third pier, Victoria Pier (later renamed South Pier), was built at South Shore in 1893. Central Pier was also known as the People's Pier because it was a popular venue for dancing.

It was in Blackpool that the first sticks of seaside rock were made, their success assured by the novelty of them having 'Blackpool' written all the way through. George Formby famously sang about his misadventures with 'A Little Stick of Blackpool Rock'.

BLACKPOOL, CENTRAL PIER 1906 53855

The end of the summer season is celebrated by Blackpool's famous illuminations, which decorate six miles of seafront. The spectacular display is billed as 'the greatest free show on earth' and, seeing it nowadays, it is hard to believe that the event began in 1912 with just eight arc lamps lighting up the promenade.

People originating from Blackpool are often called 'Sand Grown' or 'Sandgrown'uns'.

One of Blackpool's former attractions that is seen in many old photographs of the seafront was a gigantic Ferris wheel, seen in photograph 53853, below, which was constructed in 1896 beside the Winter Gardens to compete with the Tower. 30 cars, each accommodating 30 people, rose high into the air to give a spectacular view of the town. However, the wheel was a financial disaster, unpopular with visitors because every time one of the cars reached the bottom, the wheel was stopped while it was unloaded and reloaded; the structure was dismantled in 1928.

BLACKPOOL, FROM NORTH PIER 1906 53853

**BLACKPOOL
THE FLYING MACHINE
1906** 53857

In 1896 Alderman William George Bean founded Pleasure Beach, Blackpool. The 42-acre site was in the perfect spot, opposite the tram terminus, and Blackpool hoped that this new amusement park would be a big success. One of the early rides at the Pleasure Beach was one of Sir Hiram Maxim's Captive Flying Machines, shown in photograph 53857, above, which was built in 1904. Passengers sat in captive cars that revolved and swung outwards at an exhilarating 40mph, simulating flight. The Blackpool Flying Machine is still in operation and thrilling visitors at the Pleasure Beach today, virtually unchanged from Maxim's original design, and is the oldest operating amusement ride in Europe.

A modern attraction on Blackpool's seafront nowadays is a most unusual instrument, the High Tide Organ, which plays tunes in accompaniment with the tides of the sea. The organ combines hydraulics, acoustics, structural engineering, musical composition and sculpture; at high tide it is powered and operated by capturing and utilising the air pressure produced from the swell of the sea. In stormy weather the music is wild and frenzied, whilst on calmer days it is tranquil and soothing.

Blackpool's famous Tower was the idea of John Bickerstaff, mayor of Blackpool, local hotelier and entrepreneur. He was inspired by Gustave Eiffel's great tower in Paris, which had opened in 1889, and believed that a similar outstanding landmark would put the seal on Blackpool's growing reputation as a resort. Bickerstaff raised the money to construct it by calling on all the cotton barons of Burnley, Blackburn and Preston, and persuaded them to invest in the project – thus it has often been said that Blackpool Tower is built on bales of cotton. When it opened in 1891 it boasted a permanent circus, a menagerie, and an aquarium in the building at its base.

The spectacularly opulent Tower Ballroom was commissioned by John Bickerstaff a few years later, in 1899, and decorated in the French Renaissance style, modelled on the Paris Opera House. In 1956 the ballroom was gutted by fire, but was entirely rebuilt to its original designs. It was famous for its Wurlitzer organ, which featured in countless BBC broadcasts and made organist Reginald Dixon, 'Mr Blackpool Himself', a household name from 1930 until he retired in 1969. The Blackpool Tower ballroom is considered to be the spiritual home of ballroom dancing, and a highlight of the BBC TV series 'Strictly Come Dancing' is the episode that takes place there.

In 1994, to commemorate its centenary, abseiling painters highlighted the sides of the Blackpool Tower with gold. Today's holidaymakers can shudder with pleasurable vertigo as they stand on the glass floor at the top of the most iconic seaside building in the world.

In 1885, Blackpool opened the first fare-paying street-tramway in the country to be equipped with electric cars. The trams were powered by the conduit system, a positive current being carried by copper conductors in a central channel between the tracks. The Corporation took over the line in 1892 and converted it to overhead wire. A Blackpool tram played a part in TV soap history in 'Coronation Street' in 1989, when the villainous Alan Bradley was struck and killed by a tram as he was chasing Rita Fairclough across the promenade.

Another Lancashire town famous for its cakes is Chorley. Chorley cakes are fruit-filled pastry cakes, made by sandwiching dried fruit (usually currants, but sometimes raisins or sultanas) between two layers of unsweetened pastry; they are then lightly compressed with a rolling pin to be quite thin and flat. Chorley cakes are often eaten spread with butter, and perhaps with a slice of Lancashire cheese. Chorley is also famous for its two markets – the permanent Chorley Covered Market in Cleveland Street in the heart of town, and the Flat Iron Market, a traditional open-air market that takes over much of the Market Walk car park. The Flat Iron market got its name from the practice in past centuries of laying out wares flat on the ground when the market was held.

The strange building seen in photograph R309311 (below) can be found in the Rivington Country Park near Chorley. It was a pigeon tower and summerhouse, erected in 1910 for Lord Leverhulme whose fortune came from Sunlight Soap. The top room was used by Lady Lever as a sewing room, whilst ornamental doves were kept in the lower two storeys.

RIVINGTON, THE PIGEON HOUSE
c1955 R309311

ORMSKIRK, CHURCH STREET 1894 34138

In the 17th and 18th centuries the west Lancashire town of Ormskirk was famous for its clock and watchmakers. An example of an Ormskirk-made clock was bought in recent years by the National Museums and Galleries of Merseyside for £250,000. It is an amazing astronomical clock made in 1787 by Thomas Barry. It has an eight day movement and a perpetual calendar, and tells the phase of the moon, the time of sunset and the positions of the planets.

Ormskirk's parish church is unique in the north of England for having both a tower and a spire (seen in the centre distance of photograph 34138, above). The main church dates from about 1276, and the tower is actually a separate bell tower built after the Dissolution using stones from the dismantled Augustinian priory at Burscough, in which the bells that once called the monks to prayer were hung.

The genius of 18th-century Lancashire men in developing new inventions to improve the textile industry helped open the door to a new era, the Industrial Revolution. In 1733, John Kay invented his 'flying shuttle' which improved the handloom's efficiency, but this increased output capability of weavers meant faster ways of producing spun thread were needed to keep up with the demand for yarn. In the 1760s a handloom weaver at Stanhill, James Hargreaves, invented his eight-spindle 'spinning jenny' which speeded up the provision of spun wool to weavers. A few years later, Richard Arkwright's 'water frame' (a water-powered spinning machine) produced quantities of yarn strong enough to serve as both warp and weft, and in 1779 Samuel Crompton perfected the technique of spinning fine yarn with his 'mule'. The 'frames' and 'mules' were too large for use in cottages, but could be harnessed to water power, resulting in the gradual demise of the old-style cottage industries and in mills and manufactories springing up in places where there was an adequate water supply from streams. Then steam engines came along to provide even more power, resulting in the tall chimneys which were once a common sight around the mill areas of Lancashire.

From around 1815 the number of cotton factories in Lancashire expanded considerably. The mechanisation of weaving took longer to perfect, but by the mid 19th century the whole textile industry was within the factory system, and the mills were doing both spinning and weaving. Many workers at these mills were children, often pauper orphans, who worked long hours and accounted for about half the workforce. Most of the other workers were women, who did the carding and spinning. Men were mainly foremen, warehousemen and general labourers. People flocked from the countryside to the towns to work in the textile mills, initially producing woollen cloth before switching to cotton – the damp, cool climate of Lancashire was well suited to the production process of cotton yarn and cloth.

PRESTON, HORROCKSES, CREWDSON & CO LTD 1913 65593

Preston was one of the most important centres of Lancashire's cotton trade, and John Horrocks founded a textile business there that grew to be one of the biggest in the world. By the middle of the 19th century 80% of Preston's population were employed in the cotton industry. In 1842 a group of cotton workers demonstrated against poor conditions in the town's mills, and four of them were killed when troops surrounded them in front of the Corn Exchange on Lune Street and shots were fired; the event is commemorated by a sculpture on the spot. Preston was also the scene of a famous outbreak of social unrest in 1853-1854, when workers demanding pay increases were locked out of the mills by the masters in 'The Great Lock Out'. One of the reporters who came to Preston to cover the story of the lock outs and strikes was Charles Dickens, who recorded his impressions of the hardships of life in an industrial town in his novel 'Hard Times'. Although set in the fictional town of 'Coketown', it is believed to have been based on Preston.

Lancashire's cotton-weaving towns suffered badly during the 'Cotton Famine' of 1861-1865, when the blockade of the cotton-producing southern states of the USA by the north during the American Civil War prevented raw materials reaching Britain's cotton mills. Thousands of workers were made unemployed, experiencing great hardship. During the Cotton Famine many Lancashire corporations created work schemes for unemployed mill workers, using their labour to create parks and public spaces such as Williamson Park in Lancaster, and Avenham Park, Moor Park and Miller Park in Preston.

The Lancashire dialect poet Samuel Laycock worked as a power loom weaver and was laid off work during the Cotton Famine of 1861-1865. This prompted him to write his twelve 'Lancashire Lyrics', which described in local dialect verse the desperate conditions of the unemployed, and the disastrous effects the Cotton Famine had on areas dependent on the textile trades. His work is a valuable record of working people's experiences at the time. The first and last verses of 'Welcome, Bonny Brid!' movingly describe a father's love for his newborn child, despite his poverty:

> Tha 'rt welcome, little bonny brid,
> But should n't ha' come just when tha did;
> Toimes are bad.
> We're short o' pobbies for eawr Joe,
> But that, of course, tha did n't know,
> Did ta, lad?

> But though we'n childer two or three,
> We'll make a bit o' reawm for thee -
> Bless thee, lad!
> Tha'rt th' prattiest brid we han i' th' nest;
> Come, hutch up closer to mi breast -
> Aw'm thi dad.

In 1877 the solicitor Edmund Harris left a bequest of over £400,000 to Preston. One of the buildings carrying his name is the Harris Institute, but the grandest monument to his memory is the magnificent Harris Museum, Library and Art Gallery (on the right of photograph 65586 below). The relief above the portico depicts Greek philosophers and teachers, and the building has uplifting inscriptions carved on all four sides, such as 'The Mental Riches You May Here Acquire, Abide With You Always' and 'On Earth There Is Nothing Greater Than Man. In Men There Is Nothing Great But Mind'.

Many people in Preston supported the Jacobite cause (the restoration of the Stuart kings) in the 18th century. In 1745 Bonnie Prince Charlie was in Preston and declared his father (son of the deposed Roman Catholic James II) as James III in the Square. A number of volunteers from Preston and Manchester joined his army and were formed into the Manchester Regiment, but lack of support elsewhere forced the Jacobite army to turn back for Scotland and eventual defeat at Culloden. Whilst he was in Preston, Bonnie Prince Charlie gave a locket containing a portrait of himself to a local girl, Miss Pender, which is now in the Harris Museum.

PRESTON, THE SESSIONS HOUSE AND THE HARRIS MUSEUM, LIBRARY AND ART GALLERY 1913   65586

Church Street in Preston is shown in 1903 in photograph 50069,
above. The impressive church-like building on the right of the
photograph was Preston's Town Hall, designed in the Gothic style by
Sir George Gilbert Scott. Sadly, it no longer stands, as it was gutted by
a fire in 1947 and offices now stand on the site.

The Temperance Movement of the 19th century was founded in
Preston by a local man, Joseph Livesay. The word 'tee-total' was first
coined there – tradition says that it comes from when a stammering
friend of Livesay's tried to take the pledge of 't-t-total' abstinence
from alcohol. The first Temperance Hotel opened in the town, and
the first Temperance newspaper was published here, the Preston
Temperance Advocate, in 1834.

Preston had the first real piece of motorway in Britain – the Preston
Bypass which opened in 1959. The first traffic cones in Britain were
also used in building the Preston bypass, replacing the red lantern
paraffin burners which were previously used around road-works.

In the year 2002 Preston was granted the status of a city, making it
England's 50th city.

33

DARWIN, BOLTON ROAD AND INDIA MILL CHIMNEY c1955 D8026

In the 19th and early 20th centuries India was one of the British cotton industry's main customers. This fact is reflected in the name of the India Mill in Darwen, whose elaborate chimney built in the Italian campanile style still dominates the town, and is seen in the background of photograph D8026, above. The Indian leader Mahatma Gandhi visited Darwen in 1931, after accepting an invitation from the owner of a local cotton mill to come and see the disastrous effect on local industry that was being caused by India's boycott of British cotton goods as part of its bid for independence from British rule. Despite their worrying situation, Darwin's unemployed cotton mill workers are said to have greeted Gandhi with politeness and affection.

Accrington also had an important engineering industry in the 19th century. The manufacture of textile machinery, printing machinery and the Rabbeth spindle in the town gave it great prestige, as its products were exported worldwide. The Paradise Street Works made iron and tinplate products, including bedsteads and kitchen ranges, the Dowry Works produced brick-making machinery, the Ewbank carpet sweeper was manufactured by Entwistle & Kenyon, and the famous Blake's hydraulic ram was made at Oxford Street Works by John Blake. In the 1860s Accrington's Market Hall opened as a focus of the town's trade (photograph 40117, below). The extravagant carving and statuary above its entrance represent industry, commerce and agriculture.

The Haworth Art Gallery in Manchester Road in Accrington contains a fine collection of Tiffany glassware, the largest public collection of Tiffany glassware in Europe. It was presented to the town in 1933 by Joseph Briggs, a local man who left Accrington as a teenager in 1891 to seek his fortune in America. He joined the Tiffany company in New York, and eventually became its art director and assistant manager.

ACCRINGTON, THE MARKET HALL 1897 40117

Burnley takes its name from the River Brun which flows through it. Burnley's prosperity grew first from wool, and later from coal mining and cotton production, but a massive expansion took place with the completion of the Leeds & Liverpool Canal at the beginning of the 19th century, and for a time Burnley was the world's largest producer of cloth. The grand building with the dome on the left of photograph 35789 (below) is Burnley's Town Hall, opened in 1888. The central dome dominates the building, but it was originally intended that there should be a much higher tower with two flanking domes, a project that proved too expensive. The façade of the Town Hall contains a number of niches which were going to be filled with statues of Burnley's worthies, but this project was also not completed. Further down the road to its right is the building originally opened in 1855 as the Mechanics' Institute. It provided working men with educational and social opportunities, and served the town in this capacity until 1959. Since 1986 it has been Burnley's Arts and Entertainment Centre, Burnley Mechanics.

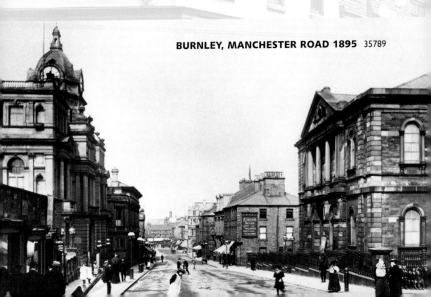

BURNLEY, MANCHESTER ROAD 1895 35789

Towneley Hall near Burnley is now a museum and art gallery but was formerly the home of the Towneley family. They were Roman Catholics and there are a number of secret 'priest holes' in the Hall that were used in the 16th century to hide priests during a period of religious persecution; one of these can be viewed through a hole in the floor of a room near the Long Gallery. In 1745 Francis Towneley led the Lancashire Jacobites who joined Bonnie Prince Charlie, but he was executed in London after the army was defeated at Culloden; his head was placed on a pike above Temple Bar, but was secretly retrieved by a family retainer and brought back to Towneley Hall, where it is now preserved in the chapel of the Hall.

South of Burnley is Bacup, home of the Britannia Coco-nut Dancers who perform their famous 'Nutters' Dance' every Easter Saturday over a route of seven miles from one side of the town to the other. The dancers perform with blackened faces, wearing breeches, skirts and plumed caps, with wooden discs, called 'nuts', attached to their hands, knees and belts. The dancers clap the 'nuts' together to make a rhythm as they move along, led by a 'whipper in' (or 'whiffler') who cracks his whip to drive away evil spirits.

NELSON, SCOTLAND ROAD AND NELSON CENTRE c1910 N146302

Nelson, north of Burnley, got its name in an unusual way. The area was originally two villages, Great and Little Marsden. When the railway arrived, because there was another Marsden a few miles up the line in Yorkshire, the station here was given the name of the nearby inn, the Lord Nelson. The station's name was then shortened to Nelson to make the sign smaller, the name stuck, and the area has been called Nelson ever since.

Beside the war memorial in Albert Road in Colne, near Nelson, is a memorial to local man Wallace Hartley. He was the bandmaster on the doomed liner 'Titanic', and kept his band playing as the ship sank in 1912 after hitting an iceberg, helping to bring calm to the desperate scene. His body was recovered from the Atlantic, still wearing his bandsman's uniform and with his music case and violin strapped around him. Over 30,000 local people turned out to pay their respects to this Lancashire hero at his funeral. He was buried in the cemetery at Colne, where his gravestone is inscribed with a violin and the music for the hymn 'Nearer, My God, to Thee' that was played by an orchestra as he was laid to rest.

5. The Lancaster Canal was known as 'the black and white canal' because it was used to transport coal ('black') to the north, and limestone and farm produce ('white') to the south.

6. The Ordnance Survey department has officially declared Dunsop Bridge, at the entrance to the Trough of Bowland, to be the village nearest to the exact centre of the British Isles. A telephone kiosk in the village marks the spot!

7. George Fox. His vision on Pendle Hill of many souls coming to Christ led him to found the religious movement he called the Religious Society of Friends, popularly known as the Quakers.

8. Burnley claims to be the 'Capital of the Pennines'.

9. During the First World War, young men from certain districts were told that if they joined up together they could serve together, in 'Pal regiments'. The 'Accrington Pals' made up the 11th (Service) Battalion (Accrington) of the East Lancashire Regiment, and also included men from Burnley, Blackburn and Chorley, and the Preston Pals became 'D' company, 7th Battalion, of the Loyal Regiment (North Lancashire). Tragically the 'Pal' system meant that large numbers of men from one area who fought together would also die together, many of whom were related. The Accrington Pals suffered terrible losses in the attack on Serre on 1st July 1916, the opening day of the Battle of the Somme, and the 'Preston Pals' were almost annihilated on 23rd July 1916, at Bazentin-le-Petite, also during the Somme Offensive. The East Lancashire Regiment, the Loyal Regiment (North Lancashire) and the South Lancashire Regiment are the forebears of the Queen's Lancashire Regiment. 'Spectamur agendo' ('Let us be judged by our acts') and 'Loyally I serve' are its mottoes.

10. The 'Stick Men' is the nickname for the men who maintain the steel structure of the Blackpool Tower.

FRANCIS FRITH

PIONEER VICTORIAN PHOTOGRAPHER

Francis Frith, founder of the world-famous photographic archive, was a complex and multi-talented man. A devout Quaker and a highly successful Victorian businessman, he was philosophical by nature and pioneering in outlook. By 1855 he had already established a wholesale grocery business in Liverpool, and sold it for the astonishing sum of £200,000, which is the equivalent today of over £15,000,000. Now in his thirties, and captivated by the new science of photography, Frith set out on a series of pioneering journeys up the Nile and to the Near East.

INTRIGUE AND EXPLORATION

He was the first photographer to venture beyond the sixth cataract of the Nile. Africa was still the mysterious 'Dark Continent', and Stanley and Livingstone's historic meeting was a decade into the future. The conditions for picture taking confound belief. He laboured for hours in his wicker dark-room in the sweltering heat of the desert, while the volatile chemicals fizzed dangerously in their trays. Back in London he exhibited his photographs and was 'rapturously cheered' by members of the Royal Society. His reputation as a photographer was made overnight.

VENTURE OF A LIFE-TIME

By the 1870s the railways had threaded their way across the country, and Bank Holidays and half-day Saturdays had been made obligatory by Act of Parliament. All of a sudden the working man and his family were able to enjoy days out, take holidays, and see a little more of the world.

With typical business acumen, Francis Frith foresaw that these new tourists would enjoy having souvenirs to commemorate their days out. For the next thirty years he travelled the country by train and by pony and trap, producing fine photographs of seaside resorts and beauty spots that were keenly bought by millions of Victorians. These prints were painstakingly pasted into family albums and pored over during the dark nights of winter, rekindling precious memories of summer excursions. Frith's studio was soon supplying retail shops all over the country, and by 1890 F Frith & Co had become the greatest specialist photographic publishing company in the world, with over 2,000 sales outlets, and pioneered the picture postcard.

FRANCIS FRITH'S LEGACY

Francis Frith had died in 1898 at his villa in Cannes, his great project still growing. By 1970 the archive he created contained over a third of a million pictures showing 7,000 British towns and villages.

Frith's legacy to us today is of immense significance and value, for the magnificent archive of evocative photographs he created provides a unique record of change in the cities, towns and villages throughout Britain over a century and more. Frith and his fellow studio photographers revisited locations many times down the years to update their views, compiling for us an enthralling and colourful pageant of British life and character.

We are fortunate that Frith was dedicated to recording the minutiae of everyday life. For it is this sheer wealth of visual data, the painstaking chronicle of changes in dress, transport, street layouts, buildings, housing and landscape that captivates us so much today, offering us a powerful link with the past and with the lives of our ancestors.

Computers have now made it possible for Frith's many thousands of images to be accessed almost instantly. The archive offers every one of us an opportunity to examine the places where we and our families have lived and worked down the years. Its images, depicting our shared past, are now bringing pleasure and enlightenment to millions around the world a century and more after his death.

For further information visit: www.francisfrith.com

INTERIOR DECORATION

Frith's photographs can be seen framed and as giant wall murals in thousands of pubs, restaurants, hotels, banks, retail stores and other public buildings throughout Britain. These provide interesting and attractive décor, generating strong local interest and acting as a powerful reminder of gentler days in our increasingly busy and frenetic world.

FRITH PRODUCTS

All Frith photographs are available as prints and posters in a variety of different sizes and styles. In the UK we also offer a range of other gift and stationery products illustrated with Frith photographs, although many of these are not available for delivery outside the UK – see our web site for more information on the products available for delivery in your country.

THE INTERNET

Over 100,000 photographs of Britain can be viewed and purchased on the Frith web site. The web site also includes memories and reminiscences contributed by our customers, who have personal knowledge of localities and of the people and properties depicted in Frith photographs. If you wish to learn more about a specific town or village you may find these reminiscences fascinating to browse. Why not add your own comments if you think they would be of interest to others? See **www.francisfrith.com**

PLEASE HELP US BRING FRITH'S PHOTOGRAPHS TO LIFE

Our authors do their best to recount the history of the places they write about. They give insights into how particular towns and villages developed, they describe the architecture of streets and buildings, and they discuss the lives of famous people who lived there. But however knowledgeable our authors are, the story they tell is necessarily incomplete.

Frith's photographs are so much more than plain historical documents. They are living proofs of the flow of human life down the generations. They show real people at real moments in history; and each of those people is the son or daughter of someone, the brother or sister, aunt or uncle, grandfather or grandmother of someone else. All of them lived, worked and played in the streets depicted in Frith's photographs.

We would be grateful if you would give us your insights into the places shown in our photographs: the streets and buildings, the shops, businesses and industries. Post your memories of life in those streets on the Frith website: what it was like growing up there, who ran the local shop and what shopping was like years ago; if your workplace is shown tell us about your working day and what the building is used for now. Read other visitors' memories and reconnect with your shared local history and heritage. With your help more and more Frith photographs can be brought to life, and vital memories preserved for posterity, and for the benefit of historians in the future.

Wherever possible, we will try to include some of your comments in future editions of our books. Moreover, if you spot errors in dates, titles or other facts, please let us know, because our archive records are not always completely accurate—they rely on 140 years of human endeavour and hand-compiled records. You can email us using the contact form on the website.

Thank you!

For further information, trade, or author enquiries
please contact us at the address below:

**The Francis Frith Collection, Oakley Business Park,
Wylye Road, Dinton, Wiltshire SP3 5EU.**
Tel: +44 (0)1722 716 376 Fax: +44 (0)1722 716 881
e-mail: sales@francisfrith.co.uk **www.francisfrith.com**